MW01493817

BODYGUARD
TO
THE ST★RS

LOOKING OVER THE SHOULDER OF HOLLYWOOD, HISTORY, AND MORE

Dr. Fred W. Campbell

ISBN: 1463597916
ISBN-13: 9781463597917

Published in the United States of America
by Motivational Speakers Institute.

Dr. Campbell is a member of the North American
Bodyguard Association.

DR. FRED W. CAMPBELL

Dr. Fred W. Campbell Awards

★ Capitol Citation Award

★ United States Presidential Service Award

★ Australia Police Olympic Gold Service Award

★ Silver Star for Bravery

★ J. Edgar Hoover Gold Medal for Public Service

★ National Life Saving Award

★ State of Arkansas Supervisor of the Year Award

★ Arkansas Governor's Award of Merit

★ National Law Enforcement Award

★ Five Governor's Quality Management Awards

★ Honorary State Police Colonel

★ Kentucky Colonel

★ Gold Medal Police Olympic Judo Champion

★ Warden's Excellent Service Award

★ Firearms Instructor Marksmanship Award

★ 2010 Supervisor of the Year Award

★ Chief of Police Citizens Award

Dedication

This book is dedicated to the men and women who daily put themselves in harm's way to protect their principal from attack.

"Greater love hath no man than this, that a man [person] lay down his life for a friend" (John 15:13).

Bodyguards must accept this statement and more. They must be willing to lay down their lives for people they may not like or even respect.

First Book

Dr. Campbell's first book, *Life's Lessons from Behind the Badge*, is available in audio and paperback versions.

Special thanks to

Janice Plyler for working on my first draft of this book. For all the hard work and caring you put into it, thanks again.

Introduction

AIR FORCE ONE

I remember standing at the Little Rock National Airport looking at the highly guarded Air Force One parked and awaiting the return of President of the United States Bill Clinton. The president was in town, and security teams from local law enforcement to the Secret Service were everywhere. I couldn't help but remember a statement that my friend, a Secret Service agent, had made to me earlier in the month.

When I heard the president would be coming to town, it reminded me of an unaccomplished goal—to tour Air Force One. Ever since my first White House detail with President George Bush, I had become fascinated with the inner workings of the Secret Service, so I called a Secret Service friend to ask if it would be possible for me to take the tour of Air Force One.

"I'd love to help you, Fred," he said, "but ever since Reagan was shot, they have tightened things up. Even I can't get on the plane if my name is not on the manifest. Fred, you know the president, you worked for him, just call him up and ask him yourself."

I did know the president of our great nation. Me, a poor old country boy who barely made it out of high school with a D in American civics! Wow! How could this happen? How did I get to know and work with such an impressive list of celebrities and dignitaries? That is one question I will answer in this book, besides revealing behind-the-scenes events with my clients and some of my own Hollywood stories and experiences and the celebrities I have met. Events that will not betray any trust of my clients, but things I think you will find interesting. I will also offer some insight into the Secret Service and what it's like to be a professional bodyguard. Later, I will also let you know if I ever made that call to the president, and if I ever got on Air Force One.

In the Beginning

I have been a chief of police, a director of training, a warden of a prison, and an executive bodyguard, but it all started for me in 1977. I was standing in the unemployment line scanning a list of jobs when I saw something that caught my eye.

"Correction Officer/Jailer. Butler County Sheriff's Office, Hamilton, Ohio/CETA."

I turned to my counselor and said, "What's this? Is this like a cop or something?"

"No, it's worse," he said. "They're looking for a jailer, and a CETA jailer at that!"

I had no idea what any of that meant, but I said that I wanted to try it. I asked if he could set up an interview for me. He indicated the job was not very desirable, so I made note that he had forewarned me. Actually, I thought this might be a cool job. Maybe I would get to wear a uniform and badge. I had worn some type of uniform my entire life, from little league baseball to basketball, wrestling to track and field (mostly field, shot put), and football. I was once a Pinkerton guard in Louisville, Kentucky.

In fact, I had tried to enlist in the navy, but they didn't want me. All I could do for them was to mop the ship. The army said I was too big and that I would have to go to Fat

9

Man's Camp. This was back in 1969 during the Vietnam War.

It's pretty bad when they won't even take you during wartime, or police action or whatever they called it.

As it turned out, my job interview was to take place the next day.

ME AT 400 POUNDS

The Interview

Human Resources people cringe when I tell this next story in my seminars. I was excited. I was to be interviewed by three people at the sheriff's office: a sergeant, a major, and a captain. I thought things were going pretty well until the major asked me a particular question.

First, let me explain that he knew from my resume that I had been a part-time youth director at my church. "Don't take this wrong," he said, "but I have had problems with church people I have hired in the past. They want to preach to the convicts and win everybody to Jesus instead of doing their jobs. I don't need that; we already have a chaplain!"

I could see right away that the major would be doing the hiring, so I said, "No problem. I'd certainly let the chaplain do his job, Jesus could do his, and I would do mine."

"Let me give you a situation," he continued, "then you can tell me how you would react. Let's say you are working in the jail and an inmate slaps you in the face. Would you turn the other cheek, like the Bible says?"

I wondered if the major was making fun of me. He did not know that I had already been asked this question by my non churched friends and that I had been fighting all my life without any problems from my church. I even taught self-defense to many women's groups. I paused just long enough to reel him in. I said, "Yes sir, I would turn the other cheek."

He came back with, "See there, that's what I mean!" looking around at the sergeant and captain with a satisfied smile.

"Yes sir, I would turn the other cheek!" I continued. "I would turn my butt cheek into his waist and then put my arm around his back and do a judo move called an O Goshi. (It's a simple hip throw.) Then I would put him in a submission hold, and if he continued to attack me, I would break his arm.

"I have a lot of Old Testament in me," I smiled.

By this time the other two had burst out laughing. "Boy, I like the way you think," the major said, "and I like your size! You're hired!

HEAVYWEIGHT CHAMPION

12

Advancement

Before long, I began advancing quickly because I had fallen in love with the job. I soon learned that the acronym CETA, Comprehensive Employment Training Act, was not looked upon as a good thing in the eyes of other deputies. CETA was enacted by Congress in 1973 as a way to help low-income people who had few job skills and needed a trade.

That sure described me: low income with few skills.

Seems the other deputies at the sheriff's office, or "real deputies," as they liked to call themselves, just put up with us CETA jailers. At least it kept them from having to work in the jail so they could go about doing "real police work" on the street.

That didn't matter to me. I got to wear a real deputy's uniform and a badge. Later, I was told that since I was doing so well, they would not only send me to jailer school but also to the police academy. After course completion, I would become a certified police officer and transfer out as a patrol officer.

Man! I couldn't believe it. Me wearing a uniform again. A real policemen. My mom was proud of me and life was good.

But I kept waiting. When was that inmate going to slap me in the face so I could show off my judo skills? I knew that I was up for the challenge.

After a couple of years on the job and after graduation from the training academy, I was asked to join the SWAT team because of my martial arts background. Next, they asked if I would be interested in teaching some of the new cadets in the academy. I felt honored to be assigned to a special school called Train the Trainers. This class taught students how to prepare lesson plans, conduct presentations, give tests, etc.

Upon graduation, I was delighted to receive a certificate from the Ohio Department of Education that stated I was certified to teach in these type schools. I couldn't believe it! Wow! A letter from ODE saying that I was a specialized teacher. Here I was, a certified teacher/trainer. If my old teachers could see me now. I wonder if this meant I could legally go into the teacher's lounge.

I have only one thing to say about the CETA program. It was one government program that worked, at least for me. CETA changed my life one step at a time. Next, I was asked if I would be interested in attending another school. All my life, I'd hated school, but now I couldn't wait for the next class and new experiences.

My Hollywood Coach

WITH LON ANDERSON

Someone had invented a new police baton, and I was asked to attend the PR 24 Baton Instructor Class. Lon Anderson was the inventor of this new baton, which reminded me of a tonfa, a legendary martial arts weapon. Lon was humble about his invention, but I recognized it as a great new weapon; it could be used far beyond just striking. It had a side handle to hold on to, which gave better control of the weapon. Another feature I liked was that it could be spun around, affording the user greater striking power if needed. It also allowed the user several more take-down moves that the old straight baton could not do.

Since I was trained by the master himself, I soon became very good with the new baton and a sought-after instructor. Anderson and I began a friendly professional relationship, and he told me about his work in Hollywood. He had taught William Shatner, of *Star Trek* fame, how to use this new baton in his new TV show, *T. J. Hooker.*

The show was based on a real-life former cop in Los Angeles. Anderson began to tell me about his Hollywood connections and suggested I look into the bodyguard business. I soon begin meeting Hollywood's rich and famous.

JAMES GARNER AND ME

Famous Bodyguards (and the Lessons I've Learned)

Bodyguard One: Frank Farmer

The first famous bodyguard we will look at is purely fictional: Frank Farmer, a.k.a. Kevin Costner. In 1992, Costner starred in the movie *The Bodyguard*. Whitney Houston starred as his client. Actually, the screenplay was written many years earlier for Steve McQueen and Diana Ross. As most good Hollywood stories go, no one would produce it, and it was rejected sixty-seven times before Kevin Costner got behind it.

The Bodyguard became the second-highest-rated movie for that year, bringing in $410 million. It was nominated for an Oscar, and Houston enjoyed $42 million in album sales.

I've enjoyed watching that movie time and time again. It includes some accurate details. The one major lesson I share with my students is to never do what Frank Farmer did: fall in love with your principal (client). Don't kiss them, dance with them, or allow them to point any sword at you.

To his credit, Frank realized this and, in the end, moved on to other clients.

There is one scene in the movie that I'm sure most people would not notice, but I did. It is the last scene of the movie. It is so compelling, in fact, that I share this scene with my students during security training.

Frank is with a new client in a large hall. The minister offers up a prayer and asks that heads be bowed. Everyone bows his or her head except Frank.

"Bingo!" I said when I noticed that Frank did not close his eyes and was fully aware of his surroundings.

You do *not* close your eyes or bow your head at any time when you are on detail. It is human nature and a sign of courtesy to bow your head when a minister prays, but in a split second anything could happen!

We will learn, in a moment, one of the key bodyguard "don'ts"—never become "part of the show."

Bodyguard Two: John Parker

When I do my seminars, I always offer people a free autographed picture if they are the first to tell me who this real-life bodyguard protected. If you work for the Secret Service, I'll bet you know who he is.

The president of the United States was in town, and he and his wife wanted to go to a play. John Parker was told to be at the White House at least an hour early so he could help escort the presidential couple to the theater. Now, John was not known in the Washington Metro Police Department for his punctuality. Again, he was late, so the chief told him to hurry to the theater and take up his post.

The president had not yet arrived at the theater, so John's tardiness would have to be dealt with later.

When the president arrived at the theater and took his box seat, John took his place behind the door. Soon, he became bored and went down into the theater to watch the play. He evidently thought the play was boring and, unbelievably, he walked to the bar next door. It is believed that he became so intoxicated that he never returned to his detail. It is assumed that he never found out until the next morning that President Abraham Lincoln had been assassinated.

John Parker was the president's bodyguard. The Secret Service had not at this time been formed. Later, Parker was brought up on charges of neglect of duty, but the charges were later dropped. Three years later he was fired for sleeping on duty and for hiring a prostitute. There is no known picture of Parker, and he seemed to drop out of sight after the last incident. He is buried in Glenwood Cemetery right outside of Washington, D.C., near a place in the park called Lincoln Circle. Now you know where the old saying in the bodyguard business comes from—"don't become part of the show." There are many lessons to be learned from John Parker. One is that you never know when you might be influencing history.

Bodyguard Three: Rosey Grier

Rosey Grier was famous for being an outstanding football player for the New York Giants in the 1960s. He has also acted in movies and was a minister.

Unfortunately, he is also known for his not-too-successful role as a bodyguard for the late Robert Kennedy. Kennedy was a presidential candidate in 1968 and was speaking on June 5 at the Ambassador Hotel in Los Angeles. Rosey, a personal friend of the Kennedys, was asked to be Kennedy's bodyguard that day. (At that time the Secret Service did not offer protection to candidates.)

Mr. Kennedy then asked Rosey to protect his wife instead of him at the Ambassador that evening. So that is what Rosey did.

That is something the Secret Service would never do. They would never leave their principal unprotected. Even a private security company would fight to stay with the client no matter what.

Rosey's plan, after the speech, was to leave the stage and go to the right; however, a former FBI agent told Rosey to go left through the kitchen, so that's what they did.

Later, Rosey would say that he heard something that sounded like a firecracker, and then he saw a group of men wrestling with a man who had a gun. He left Mrs. Kennedy and tackled the suspect, got the gun away from him, and kept him detained for the police.

Robert Kennedy would die later that evening.

Rosey Grier can't really be blamed for the tragedy. It is common practice to hire the biggest guy around for a bodyguard. (In the real world of bodyguards, one doesn't have to be big or even hold a black belt in karate.)

Fighting is the last thing a bodyguard wants to do. A bodyguard needs to learn many skills besides fighting. Rosey was just doing what a natural fighter would do. Go get the bad guy!

But did you notice, through the narration, that even though he helped apprehend Sirhan, he left his principal,

Mrs. Kennedy, unprotected?! He should have gotten her out of the building and to safety. What had happened to Kennedy was not his concern since he had been pulled by Kennedy to protect his wife. It was a terrible night for all, and, once again, a bodyguard was standing next to history.

Bodyguard Four: Trevor Rees-Jones

When I tell the following story to a group of Americans, most don't connect with the name Trevor Rees-Jones; but if you are British, I expect a ready response. It all occurred on August 31, 1997. The background was the Ritz Hotel in Paris, France. It was late in the evening, and there were the ever-present paparazzi. Trevor Rees-Jones's "principal" was an Egyptian multimillionaire named Dodi Fayed. Now are you making the connection?

Due to the endless paparazzi, Dodi Fayed asked his bodyguard, Rees-Jones, to watch closely over his girlfriend, Princess Diana. The night of the fatal accident resulted in many conspiracy theories. Since Trevor was the only survivor, he was soon interviewed and asked the question, "What do you remember about that night?"

He stated that he did remember getting into the car but had no memory after that. In Trevor's defense, he had made alternate plans to escape the press, but his boss, Dodi Fayed, changed them. Of course, Jones had no control over that.

The mistakes began when the driver, Henri Paul, showed up drunk. Trevor said he did not keep him from driving because he did not smell liquor on Paul and did not realize he was drunk.

However, according to the police report, the driver was three times over the legal alcohol limit. Being an old cop who has arrested many drunk drivers over the years, I find it difficult to comprehend that Trevor did not notice something amiss.

The next mistake was when the driver, in his inebriated state, tried to outrun the paparazzi. In the early hours of the morning, on the Pont de l'Alma underpass in Paris, three people died in a preventable accident. Trevor Rees-Jones healed physically, but he will live with that emotional trauma for the rest of his life.

Bodyguard Five: Jerry Parr

On March 31, 1981, President Ronald Reagan, former Hollywood actor turned politician, was giving a speech at the Hilton Hotel in Washington, D.C. Jerry Parr was the Secret Service agent in charge of protecting the president. As Reagan left the hotel and headed for the waiting limousine, the now infamous John Hinckley, Jr., opened fire. Agent Parr covered President Reagan and pushed him into the car as he fell on the president to protect him.

After the limo sped away, the president told Agent Parr to please get off him—he explained he thought he had some broken ribs. When Parr shifted his weight, he saw deep, dark blood foaming from the president's mouth. He knew this was far more than a broken rib, and he ordered the car to head toward the hospital.

This was a good call on Parr's part, because the president had been hit by one of Hinckley's bullets. After Reagan was assisted into the emergency room, he collapsed. The doctor later stated that if the limousine had proceeded to the White House, President Reagan would have surely died.

Agent Parr was named, and rightly so, a hero that day, but he did not consider that to be true since the president and others were shot. That, to him, was not a successful operation.

AT WORK WITH MY SECURITY TEAM

Who Uses Bodyguards?

Celebrities!

Unfortunately, people today need more protection than ever, especially celebrities who are under constant scrutiny. In past times, movie stars and jet-setters were among the many types who needed protection, but today, politicians, ministers, sports figures, and the wealthy are among the new celebrities who must be guarded.

Notables such as the Reverend Billy Graham have had to take extreme security measures, such as having his hotel rooms checked thoroughly before he enters. Scandal magazines are notorious for setting up exotic women in various stages of undress, then having them pop out of the closet with cameras rolling when the unsuspecting celebrity walks in. Pictures like these sell for millions!

Even the pope has his own Secret Service type of protection. In 1981 the pope was shot by a trained sniper. Again, in 2009, a woman jumped through the crowd and tackled the pope. In addition, famous sports figures, game show hosts, and civil rights leaders need security.

As of this writing, the latest Harry Potter movie is about to come out. Its star, Daniel Radcliffe, has already received death threats and has to be protected by private security as well as some members from the British Special Forces.

Other headliners like Beyonce, Jennifer Lopez, etc., need some type of security because of death threats or for crowd control, so they can sit down in a restaurant and have a meal in peace.

As always, celebrity comes at a price.

Politicians Do

The president of the United States has the greatest need for protection, far more than any other politician in America. One in four of our presidents has been attacked, and one out of ten has been killed. In a later chapter, I will talk more about the Secret Service and our presidents.

I will never forget the first presidential detail I worked. The president approached me on the "rope line" and asked me to do something that the Secret Service had already told me (in an earlier briefing) *not* to do. Later, I will tell you who the president was and what he asked me to do.

Governors and other state politicians often have security provided by their state police or Secret Service. Arkansas's own former Governor Bill Clinton was at one time protected by both when he was running for the presidency but was still governor of Arkansas.

The recent shooting and assassination attempt of Congresswoman Gabrielle Giffords of Arizona is a perfect example of why a politician needs a bodyguard. On the day of the shooting, there was no security. That should never have been the case.

Executives and The Wealthy

When called upon to provide security for these types of clients, it is usually not for crowd control. These clients generally need protection not only for themselves but for their families as well. It is protection from kidnapping and from death threats. This type of duty is usually long-term, twenty-four-hour, around the clock, and very expensive.

I have found these clients to be some of the best to work for as they have very little ego that needs stroking. They are used to this type of security measure and will listen to their bodyguard. They pay well and try to follow the directions for safety to a tee.

I have had the pleasure of working with one of the wealthiest men in America—billionaire Winthrop Rockefeller. I will go into detail later about my experiences with Mr. Rockefeller.

Stevie Wonder

AT WORK WITH STEVIE WONDER

When Governor Clinton became President Bill Clinton, Hollywood came to Arkansas. A large weekend event would be taking place in Little Rock. I was hired to be in charge of security for Stevie Wonder, with President Clinton being an invited guest.

Mr. Wonder wanted to be there for the entire event; he came in early so he could get a feel for things and "look" at the arena where he would be performing. My weekend with Mr. Wonder was a pleasant experience. He was one of the most personable entertainers I have worked with.

Many times these people are very magnetic in public but are completely different behind closed doors. I was with Stevie Wonder for hours on end. I spent time with him in his hotel suite. I saw and heard him interact with his staff, and he was the epitome of kindness and patience. That's not always the case with great entertainers.

Several instances stand out in my mind on that night, one amusing, but one decidedly more serious. There was, of course, a large crowd for this event. When Mr. Wonder finished his concert, he left the stage, and my protection team escorted him out of the arena. As we were walking down a long hallway packed with screaming fans, around the corner came a young woman who yelled out, "Stevie, I love you! This is for you!!" while exposing her bare breasts to him.

I was in a state of shock, and I commented, "Lady, he's blind. I appreciate what you're doing for me, but he can't see you." With that, she pulled down her blouse and started laughing.

"Oops, I forgot!" she said.

Mr. Wonder was aware that something had occurred and asked, "Chief, what happened?"

I answered, "Uh, Mr. Wonder, some woman just pulled up her blouse and showed you her breasts."

It appeared that Mr. Wonder thought about what I told him, and then with a big smile, he said, "Good!"

The second incident, I think, showed his concern for others. We had gotten him out of the arena, safely past "booby lady," and were headed up a long escalator. About halfway up, I heard a woman screaming.

"Help me!" she cried.

I quickly turned around to see a woman dressed in a long and elegant gown. The hem of her garment was being pulled down into the teeth of the escalator. Mr. Wonder asked, "What's up, Chief?!" When I quickly told him, he told me to go help her.

"I can't!" I said. Mr. Wonder was well aware of several death threats floating around that evening. Not knowing if this was merely a diversion, I got on my radio and said, "Let's go! Let's move!" So we began walking up the escalator on our own. I had to remember that Mr. Wonder might have a hard time walking the escalator, so I instructed him to take my hand as I tried to hurry my detail.

Mr. Wonder squeezed my hand and said, "No, Chief, go help the lady!" Now, all my experience told me to keep moving. You may recall earlier when I criticized Rosey Grier for leaving Mrs. Robert Kennedy to help subdue the shooter of her husband.

Fortunately, though, I had plenty of officers with me. I radioed my follow-up officer to pull off the detail long enough to hit the kill switch. By the time he reached the lady, the dress was up around her neck choking her. He hit the switch just in time. He no doubt saved this woman's life.

My job was to stay with my principal no matter what; the follow-up officer did his job, and what could have been a disastrous situation turned out well.

This business isn't play. Many times, life-and-death decisions have to be made in a split second, and the outcome will be lived with for the rest of that bodyguard's life.

Heavyweight Champion of the World
Joe Frazier

When I received the call, I couldn't believe it! The agent said, "Mr. Campbell, I would like to hire you to be the bodyguard for former heavyweight champion of the world Joe Frazier. In my mind, I wondered why in the world would Smokin' Joe Frazier need a bodyguard?

The agent told me that Joe was out of boxing and had a new career as a singer. At a recent event when Joe was walking onto the stage, a heckler yelled out that famous quote of Howard Cosell's from the Frazier-Foreman fight ("Down goes Frazier, down goes Frazier!")

Frazier then commenced to single out the heckler and pound his head. The agent added, "This guy is now suing us. I don't need you to protect Joe from the world; I need you to protect the world from Joe!"

Now, this was a first for me, as I had never had a request quite like this. I added, as a little joke, "Who should I send the bill to—Joe or the world?"

He answered simply, "We will pay for it." I never even heard him chuckle. I guess that's why I am not a comedian.

The event, however, went well. As I was in the dressing room with the champ, he seemed in high spirits and ready for his show. I was to drive him from the dressing room to the stage in a golf cart.

On the brief trip he began talking to me, and I told him how much I respected him, and that it was an honor for me to be there. I advised him that if he heard anything that bothered him to let me handle it and for him to just enjoy the applause.

"Oh, they told you about last week," he said.

"Yes, I heard something about it," I answered.

"Well, I'll do my best. That stuff just drives me crazy!"

Actually, the evening went well. Joe Frazier, heavyweight champion, sang his heart out, and the crowd went wild. Since there were no major incidents, the "world" was saved one more night from Smokin' Joe Frazier.

I felt like a superhero—protector of the world.

Lessons Learned

I believe I learned a great deal from both these stars. Both men had endured hardships. Mr. Wonder has been blind from birth, but he never lets this stop him from achieving the highest acclaim in the music world. Randy Jackson of American Idol stated, "Stevie Wonder is the greatest singer/songwriter the world has ever known."

Joe Frazier, who was raised in the toughest of neighborhoods, never let that obstacle stop him from his dream. I often use a film clip in my seminars of the fight where George Foreman knocks Joe down six times, and Howard Cosell yells, "Down goes Frazier, down goes Frazier!"

Joe did go down, but he kept getting up, and although he lost the fight, he never stayed down. I tell my students that we all face failure and disappointment in life. Being knocked down isn't the same as being knocked out. Smokin' Joe Frazier is an inspiration to others who get knocked down in life. You don't have to stay down; you still have enough fight in you to get up again.

Joe would later come back and win other fights. In fact, I'm told he made more money after that fight than he made in his entire career before the Foreman fight.

Protecting the Presidents
and Other High-Security Clients

RECEIVING AN AWARD FROM GOVERNOR MIKE HUCKABEE

The Secret Service has the responsibility of protecting the president of the United States. Abraham Lincoln, at the time of his death, had on his desk a bill to create this agency. It was finally commissioned on July 5, 1865, but it was not until 1901, after the assassination of President McKinley, that the Secret Service began protecting the presidents.

Prior to this, the agency's responsibility was to suppress counterfeit currency, mail robbery, bootleggers, etc. The title of "Secret Service" stemmed from agents who wanted their identities kept secret so they could infiltrate the underground without being known.

I was called into the captain's office and told I was to be one of the deputies assigned to work with the Secret Service. I found that the assignment was to help protect President George H. W. Bush. The following week, the president would be speaking at a local college in Ohio. I felt honored and looked forward to a briefing with the Secret Service agents.

The Briefing

When I arrived, I knew something was up. There seemed to be a lot of hush-hush talk going on with the agents. We all were seated, and the lead agent began the briefing. We were then informed that there was a serious death threat on the president's life.

Now, this happens all the time, but this one was being looked into more closely. We were told to stay focused on the president. "Do not," the agent said, "*become part of the event!* Do not ask him for his autograph, do not speak to him, and do not shake his hand. You are there to work."

The briefing went on for some time, and then we were given our assignments. I would be close to the limousine. When the president exited the car, I was to watch the crowd and stay with the car while he gave his speech. I had been told not to worry and that an agent would be close by if I had any questions.

The agents, of course, had been working on this event for some time. On the day of the event, the bomb-sniffing dogs went through the arena again, and everyone was on high alert. I got to my post at the prescribed time and waited for the president to arrive.

Suddenly, I heard a loud noise coming from the sky. Three helicopters went flying overhead, a white one in the middle of two green ones. I looked immediately to my assigned agent and said, "Well, there he is!"

"Who?" he said.

"The president!"

"Oh," he answered, "which helicopter is he in?"

"The white one in the middle, of course."

"If you were to try and shoot it down, that's the one you would aim at, right?" Yes, I guess would.

"So, he was on one of the green ones, wasn't he?"

He just smiled. In a few minutes, I heard that loud noise again. I looked up and saw two white helicopters and a green one.

"Who is that?" I asked.

"That's the president."

"But I thought the other group of helicopters was the president."

"That's what I wanted you to think!"

I decided not to ask him which one the president was in from this group of helicopters. I had already fallen into that trap once.

In a little while, I could see in the distance a large group of blue lights flashing. The presidential motorcade was about to arrive. I couldn't believe all the vehicles—police cars, SWAT vans, ambulances—the line went on and on. Toward the front, three presidential limos pulled up close.

The excitement of the crowd was contagious, and I must admit that I was also pretty pumped up. There was one car in the middle, slightly head of the others, and two more by its side.

Agents jumped out of the lead car and took up a point at each corner where they stood patiently. Finally, I said to my agent-partner, "Will he be getting out soon?"

"Who?" he asked. (Oh, here we go again.)

"The president," I said.

He looked at me and smiled. "Which car is he in?"

"The black limo."

"Which one? There are three black limos."

"Okay," I said, falling into his trap once more, "I assume he will get out of the one surrounded by the agents."

"That's exactly what I wanted you to think."

Then suddenly the president jumped out of the last car, and the agents quickly surrounded him.

"Well, you got me again," I said.

The agent just smiled and said, "We don't always do this much cloak and dagger, but with a serious death threat we like to mix it up a little."

The president started heading toward the crowd, and everyone started shouting, "Mr. President, Mr. President, over here, over here!!"

He was supposed to go straight to the event, but as all presidents do, he couldn't resist the screaming crowd. That was fine. I was keeping a close eye on the crowd when, all of a sudden, the president did something out of the ordinary. I could see him heading straight for me. He stopped in front of me and put his hand out to shake mine.

I just knew this was another secret service test. I'd already flunked two today by picking the wrong helicopter and the wrong limousine. I remembered the briefing: "Don't become part of the event!" What was I to do? The president of the United States wanted to shake my hand.

I just stood there looking into his face when he did something that made me lose all my Super Secret Service training. He said my name.

"Fred," he said, "Barbara and I want to thank you for being out here today. I'm sure you had other things you could have been doing."

With that, I broke down, put my hand in his, shook it, and said, "Thank you, Mr. President. It is an honor to be here today!"

Afterwards he moved on, and I realized that not only did I shake his hand, but I spoke with him as well. "I'm toast," I thought to myself. "I'm FRT (fired right there)!" I slowly turned to my Secret Service buddy and said, "I'm so sorry! Am I fired?"

He laughed, "No! You did just fine! I had your back."

"You know what? He knew my name? Who told him? Did he ask who that good-looking deputy was?" I joked, realizing I was not in hot water. (My head must have been swollen to twice its size by then.)

"No, Fred, I hate to burst your bubble, but he read the name tag on your uniform."

"Oh," I said, a bit deflated. "I didn't even think of that."

With that, I resumed duties and can proudly say that the rest of the day went fine. The president gave his speech and arrived home safely. That evening as I lay in bed, I thought back on the day. I had just met and helped protect

the president of the United States. He shook my hand and thanked me personally, even if he did read my name tag. "Aaah!" I thought. "I worked with one of the finest law-enforcement agencies in the world," the Secret Service.
Not bad for a poor old CETA worker

Best Wishes to Chief Fred Campbell

PRESIDENT BUSH

Would You Take a Bullet?

I get asked all the time, and I know the Secret Service does as well, "Would you take a bullet for the president? Would you take one for your client?"

One of my Secret Service friends answered this question for me this way: "My job is to keep the president out of those types of situations where they might occur. If it does occur, and it is necessary, the answer would be yes."

I feel the same way. If needed, I would put my life on the line for a client. That's why I don't take every job I'm offered. If I wouldn't lay down my life for that client, he needs to find protection elsewhere.

In a private protection business, I have that luxury. If a person is an agent of the Secret Service, however, his badge covers everyone the agency protects. If a person can't take a bullet, he should never apply for the job.

Agent Tim McCarthy

Secret Service Agent Tim McCarthy was working the detail in 1981 at the Hilton Hotel the day President Reagan was shot. He had been on presidential protection detail for a number of years before this tragedy occurred.

In my seminars, I show the actual video taken of this assassination attempt. Agent McCarthy heard the gunfire and turned his body sideways to better protect the president. The footage then reveals McCarthy being hit by the bullet intended for the president. As McCarthy fell from the shot by John Hinckley, agent Jerry Parr (the lead agent I mentioned earlier) pushed the president into the limo.

Parr said that agent Tim McCarthy was the real hero that day. He took the bullet, without hesitation, for President Reagan. McCarthy, at this writing, is only the fourth agent in the history of the Secret Service to have taken a bullet for a president.

President Clinton

GOVERNOR BILL CLINTON AND I, AT A LAW ENFORCEMENT NEWS CONFERENCE

The next president I worked with after President Bush was my former governor, Bill Clinton. I worked for him for what seemed like forever. I know that when talking or writing about political figures, what is said or written can cause controversy, so I will try stay away from political issues.

I will only discuss my working relationships with all of them. In presidential or government protection, one must put all personal convictions aside and focus on the job at hand.

When I first met Bill Clinton, we both still had dark hair. He was called the Boy Governor because of his boyish looks and young age. At that time, I was applying for the job of training director for the state's largest training academy, the Arkansas Department of Correction and Parole Training Academy.

Since I was asking for a higher salary than was advertised (due to my past law enforcement and training experience), I had to get special permission from the governor's office. Permission was granted, and I was later told that the governor probably didn't even see the request; someone in another agency probably approved it. But, I later heard that it was he who approved it, and I liked that thought better!

I immediately went to work, and it was not long before I began serving on various committees for the governor. I was chairman of the training committee that was in charge of special management training for fifty thousand state employees. I became an advisor for quality management for our agency and then for all law enforcement.

Soon I was invited to the mansion, where Governor Clinton always called me by name even though I had on no name tag. I felt especially honored until I discovered his amazing memory for all names. It has been said that he could meet a person once and remember the name forever. That was part of his charm and success. I think it had a lot to do with his immense popularity in Arkansas and the fact that he was reelected for president of the United States. Bill Clinton could make you feel like he had known you for years.

Basically, Bill Clinton was just a smart, good old country boy who caught a break in politics. He never failed to ask how your mother was or some other personal question. A person couldn't help but like him. He is one of the hardest workers I've ever known. He could go without sleep for days. I remember walking into a large meeting hall where I was scheduled to speak before he did. He was leaning up against a door watching the crowd.

I spoke briefly with his security detail; I had trained many of them, so we chatted "cop stuff" before I asked permission to speak to the governor. I knew it would be okay, but this was not my detail, and I respected their position.

"Sure," they responded, "he would love to hear from you!"

I walked over to him and said, "Good evening, Governor." And before I could introduce myself, he said, "Fred, I see you are speaking tonight before me."

"Yes sir, I'm your opening act!"

"Great!" he laughed. "Liven them up for me!"

When I glanced at him, he looked worn out. There were dark circles under his eyes, and he was leaning on the door frame so heavily I was afraid he might fall down. "You okay, Governor?" I asked.

"There's been a lot going on, and I haven't slept for several days," he said, "but I'll be okay. I really appreciate what you said in the meeting the other day, and I wanted you to know it."

I couldn't believe he even remembered.

I surely did, because it was one of those rare times that I saw the famous Clinton temper. There was a large group of us in his conference room, and he was going around the room asking for updates from the teams on quality management. QM was one of his pet projects, and he had decided that Arkansas would be one of the first states to go for total quality management.

This meant that we would be a customer-driven state, and the mission of the state would be to deliver excellence in customer service to its citizens. The meeting wasn't going well for Clinton because no one was giving him answers that he could use in his next news conference. He became red in the face and yelled, "This is not what I want. Has no one been listening?! I want results!"

He then turned to me and yelled, "Fred (this time I was not glad he remembered my name), what do you have?!" I knew what he wanted. He wanted to be able to tell the media that this new plan of his in quality management was working and saving the state money.

"Governor," I said, "our law enforcement team has come up with a proposal that will save the state thousands of dollars and will keep the purchasing of our products here in Arkansas. I found that all of the various law enforcement agencies are purchasing their ammunition and targets from various companies, mostly from outside Arkansas.

"Sir," I continued, "we have one of the largest ammunition plants in America right here in Arkansas—Remington Arms! Why can't we buy all the ammunition and targets from them? This will save the state thousands of dollars and will keep the purchasing of our products in Arkansas. They said they would give us a better price than anyone else, and our money would stay right here!"

His face lit up. "That's what I'm talking about, Fred! You and your team did a great job! Get that on my desk and keep ideas like that coming. If I can ever be of help to you, let me know!"

Remember in the introduction of this book how I wanted to go aboard Air Force One at Little Rock National Airport? In that moment, the president's words came back to me.

As the agent from the Secret Service had said, "Fred, you know the president. Ask him."

After all, I thought, he did tell me to call him if I ever needed anything. I guarantee that if I had called him, he would have remembered my name and the incident at the state conference meeting, and he would probably have said yes. But, as I began to think about it, I knew he had more important issues to deal with—stateside, internationally, and personally.

Therefore, I lost my chance to board Air Force One, and I know he would also have asked about my mother, but I just did not want to bother him.

Looking back, I don't think most Arkansans, even Bill himself, thought he would be elected president of the United States. He even told close friends that he was just running to get his name known for the next election. When he did win, I was invited to the Inaugural Ball, as many in Arkansas were. Since I was sure he would be only a one-term president, I did not speak with him about going to Washington with him in some Law Enforcement position. If he had asked me, I would have said yes, then I would have given up my job in Arkansas, and if he lost the next election I would have been job hunting again. So I just stayed put.

It was just a matter of time, I thought, before some skeletons would come out of the closet. It was common knowledge that Mr. Clinton had certain problems. I have friends who have been on his security team, and I know certain things. I have been involved in his security at a local level, and I try not to speak out of turn negatively about him or any other client. That's not what I was paid to do. My loyalty is not for sale, but many of President Clinton's issues are now public knowledge.

44

When several agents from the Secret Service were sub-poenaed to testify against President Clinton, they refused to cooperate with Congress when they requested personal information about the president. They refused, and I agree with that decision. Unless the agents had knowledge of illegal acts or issues that affect National Security, they should have remained silent. The agents held out for as long as they could but they were later ordered to talk.

*SHAKING HANDS WITH SECRET SERVICE AGENT
IN CHARGE JOHN COOK*

Former assistant U.S. Attorney General Webb Hubbell.

AT WORK WITH WEB HUBBLE

Former U.S. Assistant Attorney General Web Hubble

I knew of Web Hubble from his earlier days in Arkansas where he was a football star. At one time, he was the mayor of Little Rock. He was also an Arkansas State Supreme Court Justice and law partner with Hillary Clinton and Vince Foster. President Clinton carried him to D.C. and appointed him assistant U.S. attorney general. Mr. Hubble had led a charmed life, but the day I met him was not a social call.

The U.S. Marshal had delivered him to me. I was in charge of his security for a few hours: He had been sentenced to twenty-one months in a federal prison for cheating his former clients at the Rose Law Firm in Little Rock. The amount was over $500,000. He was in handcuffs when we "met." The courts had ordered him to speak to my cadets at the Correction Academy. After taking off his handcuffs, I started to shake his hand and then remembered he was an inmate. (I never shake an inmate's hand until the day that person is released.) Shaking hands is a sign of friendship, a welcome, or a departing gesture. Mr. Hubble did not yet fall into any of those categories.

I asked Mr. Hubble, after he was seated in my office, what he intended to tell my cadets. He simply stated that he would brief them on how he got caught up in this unethical trap. He told me that it had started out slowly when he borrowed money from a fund and then he would pay it back. Then he would repeat the action but this time would not pay it back. Next, he stated he would charge clients for work not done. He admitted he knew it was wrong, but after a while the amount grew into something he could not repay.

"I'm so ashamed," he said, "and I have lost everything! The first night I was prison, the other inmates yelled at me, 'Judge Hubble, you put me in here! I'll get you!' 'You might as well take off your underwear because I'm going to hurt you!' I couldn't believe I was actually there. I will tell your cadets that corruption always starts small. Then it gets too big to get out of."

At this, Hubble began crying, so I tried to change the subject until one of my staff came in and said they were ready for his speech. He spent the whole day with me, as he had been ordered to speak to several groups of inmates as well. When I returned him to the marshals that day, I shook his hand, as I would not be seeing him again. I wished him well and tried to encourage him.

As he was taken from my custody, I couldn't help but think about one thing he said. "I'm so ashamed. I just wish I could move to some island and sell T-shirts on the beach. Somewhere where no one knows me."

I tell all my law-enforcement classes the Web Hubble story. The price of corruption has a price too high to pay, because, at some point, the devil comes looking for his pay, and he always collects with hellish interest rates.

Civil Rights

DAISY BATES, ROSA PARKS, MY SECURITY TEAM AND I

The two foremost women in the civil rights movement have been Rosa Parks and Daisy Bates. Movies have been made about both these fine ladies, and I have had the privilege of protecting them both.

Driving Ms. Daisy

One day I received a call requesting my services for a large birthday party. Ms. Daisy Bates, who led the Little Rock Nine into Central High School in Little Rock, Arkansas, in 1957 and commanded national attention for the desegregation of schools in the South, was turning eighty. A huge party was planned with people coming from all around the world, including the president of the United States.

I assumed I was needed for crowd control at the event and perhaps to accompany her to an autographing session for her latest book. Of the many invitations sent out, one was returned with a death threat. I could not conceive that anyone would want to harm this woman, so highly esteemed by every president since Dwight D. Eisenhower. She was close friends with Martin Luther King, Jr., and President Bill Clinton. Because I knew the president would probably be there, I gave the returned invitation and death threat to friends of mine in the Secret Service.

Now, as I was gathering up a team for this event, Ms. Bates asked me who was going to be her personal bodyguard. I told her I was trying to find a retired African-American Secret Service agent.

"What's wrong with you doing it?" Ms. Bates asked.

"Well," I explained, "I just thought that since this will make international news, you'd want your closest protection to be African-American."

I will never forget the look on her face. She said, "Fred, do you think I am prejudiced?"

"No, of course not, I just thought…"

"Well, that settles it. I want you."

Of course, I was proud to protect Ms. Bates and did it with the help of a great staff.

When we got into the limo, I looked over at her and said, "Ms. Daisy, I'm so sorry people send you letters like the invitation today. I promise you one thing, I will give my life for you tonight if needed."

"Oh, honey," she said, "let's hope that doesn't happen. They haven't shot out my windows in years!" She then leaned over and kissed me on the cheek.

The evening had been long, and I was nervously anticipating problems. Thankfully, there were none. Except during dinner, when Ms. Daisy confided in me that she hated the food. She said, "After this is over, will you take me to get something to eat?"

When we left the arena to go home, I asked her if she was still hungry. "Oh, yes!" she said. "And I know right where I want to go!"

Every time I pass that restaurant on Broadway Avenue in Little Rock, I am reminded of my good friend Ms. Daisy Bates. Where did the limo go at her direction? Wendy's!!

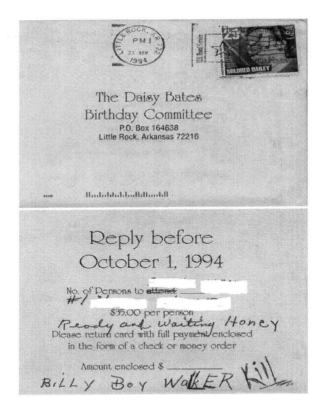

DEATH THREATS

Rosa Parks

GOVERNOR TUCKER, MS. PARKS AND I

Ms. Rosa Parks is better known internationally than Ms. Daisy. At her death she was the only woman who had ever lain in state at the Capitol in Washington, D.C. Ms. Parks, of course, made international news when she refused to give up her seat to a white man on a city bus in Montgomery, Alabama, in 1955.

Academy Award winner Angela Bassett starred in the movie simply titled *The Rosa Parks Story.* I had my team meet her at the airport, and I would later touch base with them at the hotel. That was several days before Ms. Bates's birthday celebration.

When I met her face to face, I thought, "How could anyone so tiny and fragile change history?" But, she sure did!

I began talking to her and trying to assess what her threat level was. She said there had been no death threats lately. Her aide left us alone for a while, and I told her how much I admired her bravery in not giving up her seat on the bus those many years ago.

"Bravery?" she raised an eyebrow. "Oh, I don't know about that. I knew I was making a stand for civil rights, but I was so tired after being on my feet all day that all I wanted to do was sit down. I wasn't going to give up my seat for no white man, no black man, or nobody else!"

I was always under the assumption that she had been sitting in the front of the bus where the whites normally sat, but, in fact, she was sitting in the rear of the bus, where blacks sat, when the incident occurred. The bus was crowded, and the white man felt she should give up her seat to him. She was just trying to get home and could not take this last demand on her dignity any longer!

Later, I read that after she had left my event, her apartment was ransacked and she was assaulted. "How could anyone do something like that to such a sweet old lady?" I said to myself. When I read of her death, and that she would lie in state at the U.S Capitol Rotunda, I thought, "Finally, Ms. Rosa, you can truly rest in peace."

Hollywood

MY ATTILA THE HUN IMPERSONATION

I may not be a stunt double for Brad Pitt, but, I have been told that I favor Max Baer, Jr.'s "Jethrine Bodine" character from The Beverly Hillbillies. Actually, I conduct a seminar dressed as Attila the Hun and present a management class based on the bestselling book called *Leadership Secrets of Attila the Hun,* by Wess Roberts.

When the A&E miniseries *Attila the Hun* was being conceived, I just knew I had a chance to play the part of Attila, but somehow that didn't work out. My movie career would have to come later. I do remember, however, when

54

I first felt like a star. It was when I was first asked for my autograph. I was walking to a seminar in full Attila costume when this young boy came running up to me in the lobby of this large hotel.

"Sir," he said, "can I please have your autograph?"

I could just feel my head swelling when I answered, "Sure, son!" I then signed his paper "Best Wishes from Fred Campbell, aka Attila the Hun."

"Thank you, sir!" he said with a big smile. I watched him head back towards his mother. All of a sudden he looked down at the autograph, then back at me, then said, "Hey, you ain't Weird Al Yankovic!" and threw down the autograph and took off running.

Oh, well, so much for my first autograph seeker.

There was another funny event that occurred while I was Attila. The event had no dressing room facilities, so I showed up and stayed in full costume until I returned home that evening. I finished speaking, and on my way home from the event, I stopped by a local Convenience Store, to buy some breath mints, so I dropped in at a local business that sold food and gas.

Behind the counter was a very portly lady who perked up and asked, "Who are you?!"

"I can't tell you," I said with a smile.

"What are you doing here?" she jovially questioned.

Again, I answered, "I can't tell you!"

"Ahh!" she said, "You're an undercover cop acting like a hooker!"

At that, I began laughing. "I can't tell you," I said again.

"Oh, honey!" she said with a big belly laugh (and she had plenty to laugh with). "If some man tries to pick you up, come back and tell me, then I'll know there's still hope for me, 'cause you are the ugliest woman I've ever seen!"

I've had lots of fun performing as Attila, but so far I've not required personal protection services to keep the fans away.

BACKSTAGE WITH MY "HUNNETS"

My First Movie

MY FIRST MOVIE, "THE GREAT OBSESSION"

My debut as an actor dates back to the '80s. A Hollywood studio came to Arkansas looking for a location for their next movie. They, of course, made it sound like it would be a shoo-in for the next Academy Awards. The title was *The Great Obsession.* I was chosen to play a tough chief of police. I thought it was a bit of typecasting since that really was my profession, but I went along with the creative flow.

Filming began for me at the scene of a car accident. There had been a horrible crash, and standing next to me was my detective (who, by the way, I am told was the same stunt actor who fell through the ceiling for Sylvester Stallone in the first *Rambo* movie). So I guess this was his first big speaking part.

Underneath the blanket lay a man who had died during the crash. The victim had been under investigation. One of my lines in the movie, if I remember correctly, was, "Do you really believe this was an accident?"

Do you know how many times I repeated that line?!

That brief scene took about five hours to shoot. A man came running from the car on fire. After he fell to the ground, they stopped filming, put the flames out on the stunt man, and replaced him with a dummy under the blanket.

The fire scene took forever; it seemed like something was always going wrong—not enough fire, not enough sound, and my speaking part had to be shot over and over. I was not loud enough, then too loud, then a plane flew over, and we had to do it all over again.

It was a lot of work and not much fun, but the day finally came when we gathered to watch the first cut of the movie. The movie began, and all was going well until the star of the show was in his bedroom and was eventually joined by three beautiful women who traipsed around in various forms of dress.

Did I say dress?! I meant undress!

None of us (actors) remembered this scene, and we began to gasp and protest. After all, we had bragged about the movie and promoted it locally.

What would my wife and children think? And what about my mother!?

We local actors complained to the filming company and reminded them of our agreement not to film any nude scenes in Arkansas. They frankly replied that they did not break the agreement; those scenes were filmed in Hollywood!

In the credits, they listed all our names, including the three women in the bedroom scene, who were, by the way, the last three titleholders of Ms. USA Nude Woman. Thank goodness it went right to video, I was told, and I don't know a soul who has a copy.

My next Hollywood venture came a few years ago. I received a call from the TV shows *Cold Case Files* and *Hard Copy.* They were both interested in doing a TV show about two different cases of mine.

The initial story was in my first book, titled *Life's Lessons from Behind the Badge.* Donald Korn was a brutal mass murderer and was being held in the Butler County Jail where I was a young correctional officer. I won't relate the whole story, as I have told it in my last book, but inmate Korn was leaving the county jail in a few days for death row, where he was sentenced to die in the electric chair. He tried to escape one night while I was on duty but failed in his attempt, and I had a major role in keeping him from escaping. For some reason he liked me, and I got to know him pretty well.

Years later, his sentence was overturned. It was determined, though, that he may have been involved in several other murders. When I received a call from the A&E network, they asked for pertinent information on Donald Korn. I gave them all the information I had on the case, then recommended they speak to my friend, Detective Frank Smith, who was the head of the Cold Case Division at the Sheriff's Office. He was really the one they needed to speak to. (I had moved out of the state and had been out of the loop for years.)

They did indeed contact Smith, and A&E did the story called *A Killer Named Korn.* You can see this episode (which can be ordered from A&E *Cold Case Files*) and then read my story in my first book, *Life's Lessons from Behind the Badge.* In the story called "Death Row Religion," you will see a complicated man and you will learn why he did not kill me the night of his attempted escape.

Later, I received a call from the producer of the TV show *Hard Copy.* They were looking at a case that was still under investigation, in some people's view. It was back in the '80s, when I was the chief of police in Brinkley, Arkansas. A novel of fiction based on this case had been published, and many people believed the novel was factual.

Hard Copy wanted to prove that the wrong man was convicted and the killer was still on the loose. I gave them the information but reminded them that the sheriff's office had made the arrest, not the city police, so they would have more information than I.

Both experiences with these networks were interesting, and I enjoyed working with them; however, *Hard Copy* eventually seemed to lose interest in the project.

Luke, I Am Your Father!

Twice in my bodyguarding career, I have said, "*He* needs a bodyguard?" The first was Joe Frazier, heavyweight champion of the world. The second was David Prowse. Does that name ring a bell? No? Well, how about the name Darth Vader? Yes, Mr. Evil himself.

Why in the world would Darth Vader need a bodyguard? His agent said it was for crowd control. The kids could get rough.

I decided to take the gig since he was coming to this large amusement park. I found Mr. Prowse to be a gentle giant. He stood at six feet, seven inches and weighed about 275 pounds—without the boots.

Prowse revealed that there were three actors who played Darth Vader; however, he did the hard work—wearing that heavy suit and playing the entire sword-fighting scene with Luke Skywalker. James Earl Jones did the voiceover, and that rich baritone was perfect since Prowse's voice was a high-pitched British accent.

The actor Saba Shin Shaw was in a short scene where Darth Vader is seen as a ghostlike figure. Surely it seemed as if Prowse should have been rewarded with this memorable scene, but that was not in the cards. It was easy to read between the lines about the animosity between Mr. Prowse and the producer, George Lucas. For one thing, he told the crowd that Lucas did not tell him what the lines were when it came to the now-infamous scene where Vader says, "Luke, I am your father!" He wanted the lines kept secret.

Prowse also told the crowd that night that he had been offered the role of Chewbacca, but when he was told he was expected to wear the heavy, furry costume in addition to wearing the heavy mask, he declined.

Instead, he chose the role of Darth Vader, thinking surely he could take the mask off. That did not happen for him. The evening went well. There were some boos when he first came out on stage, and a few kids seemed to want to kick him or try to push him over as he walked around, but I kept him safe and the Empire lived on.

I enjoyed working with Prowse—a.k.a. Darth Vader—and wish him well.

Autographs

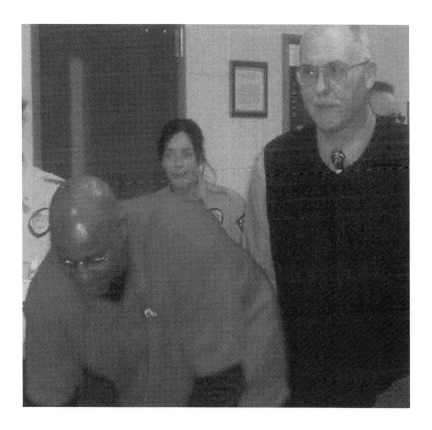

FIVE TIME NBA ALLSTAR, SYDNEY MONCRIEF AND I

One of the services I offer my clients is to be the bad guy. Celebrities go through stages of autograph signing. Phase one: They will sign anything, anytime they are requested. It's all new to them and they can't believe people want their autograph. Phase two: They wonder why people want their autograph. They have made it now and autographs are a necessary evil. They appreciate the request but would really rather not be bothered, although they will do it in limited situation. Phase three: They can't believe no one wants their autograph. They are on the decline in their career and can't believe the public dosen't love them anymore. The best time, of course, to get an autograph is in phase one or three. I always get with my clients and inquire how they want to handle autographs. I explain I will be the bad guy if they want to limit autographs. Here is how it works .

My client has told me he only wants to sign about five autographs but he doesn't want to look like he is an SOB. So this is what happens. When we get to the fifth autograph seeker, I tap him on the shoulder and (declare, just loudly enough for everyone to hear), "Sir, they're expecting you down at the arena. I think we had better go." He then looks at the crowd and then back to me and says, "Sorry, guys, I've got to go. I can't argue with the man with the gun (I may not even have a gun, and of course I don't smile). Thanks, everyone, thanks for coming today." We then leave for the event and everyone hates me.

The worst time to ask for an autograph is when the celebrity is dining. Please don't rush up to him or her while he or she is eating. If I see this coming, I will try to stop the autograph seeker very quietly and tell him or her, "Mr. Pitt would like to finish eating and he would love to talk to you afterwards if you don't mind. Of course, it may be awhile before he is finished." I then give them my business card and tell them to write me and I will get Mr. Pitt to send them a signed, autographed photo, addressed just to them. This usually works, and then I always follow through on my promise.

EVEN I HAD TO HAVE THIS AUTOGRAPH. I'M AN OLD TREKKIE

AS CRUISE SHIP FEATURED SPEAKER, PRESENTING MY "BODYGUARD TO THE STARS" SEMINAR.

Actor Rick Dial

WITH ACTOR RICK DIAL

Rick Dial has been in more Academy Award movies than anyone I have known. He has starred in *Sling Blade, The Apostle,* and *Crazy Heart,* all Academy Award winners. He also has been in *Secondhand Lions, The General's*

Daughter, The Badge, Come Early Morning, Beyond the Wall, and *Mumford,* among other notable films.

But when I met Rick Dial some years ago, it was not on a movie set. I had just moved my family to Malvern, Arkansas, to take a new position, and we were looking for a church to attend.

One Sunday morning we went to services at the First Baptist Church, and I noticed a man who looked very familiar up on the platform singing. I asked a man about him, and he said, "Oh, he gets that all the time. He and Billy Bob Thornton are good friends—they both grew up here in Malvern. He was in Billy Bob's movie *Sling Blade.*"

One day as I was setting up a security escort for him, I asked if he would agree to an interview for an article I was writing.

I found Rick Dial to be a very humble man. I began to praise him for his film work, but he just smiled and gave the credit to others. The interview started with his friendship with Billy Bob Thornton. They both had moved to Malvern when they were teenagers. He noticed that Billy Bob was a little different for a small town, and he wasn't making any friends at school. His mom was accused of being a witch. (She actually read palms.)

He said that he was always for the underdog, so he became friends with Thornton. Even though they seemed different, they had two common interests—music and baseball. They remained good friends until Thornton moved away.

When he started shooting his soon-to-be Academy Award-winning movie *Sling Blade*, Billy Bob called and said, "Man, I've got this little movie I'm shooting in Arkansas, and I've got a part for you." Dial told me, "I couldn't believe it. I said, 'I'm a furniture salesman, not an actor.' "

Thornton would not take no for an answer, so Dial accepted the offer.

"What was it like?" I asked.

"At first, it was fun, but after a while it was just a lot of sitting around waiting for someone to come and get you or just waiting for the weather to change! We shot it and waited for the movie to come out. It started getting great reviews, and there was talk of it being in the running for an Oscar.

"Well, the rest is history, and *Sling Blade* is now one of the most acclaimed films to have ever come out of Hollywood. Especially if you like mustard on your biscuit."

After that, the movie roles for Dial started coming in. Robert Duvall had had a small part in the movie *Sling Blade*, and he asked Billy Bob, "Who is that fat guy in the movie, and who is his agent?"

"Billy Bob told him, 'He ain't got no agent—he's just a furniture salesman from my hometown in Malvern, Arkansas.'

"For some reason the seasoned actor Duvall had taken a liking to me," continued Dial, "and he called me in about a week and asked me to be in his upcoming movie, *The Apostle.* Then later I received a call from Paramount Pictures to be in the movie *The General's Daughter,* starring John Travolta. I really wanted to do the movie, but I was out of vacation time at work. I went to my boss, Mr. Orr, and he had just finished reading the book."

Mr. Orr said, "Man, this could be a great opportunity for you, Rick! Let me think about it."

Dial continued, "That very evening I got a call from Robert Duvall. He said, 'Ricky, I hear Paramount wants you in *The General's Daughter.*' When I told him that I had used up all my vacation days, he insisted on calling my boss, and so he did. Duvall said, 'Hey, man, this is Paramount's big picture of the year—you can't turn this down!'

"So the rest is history, Mr. Campbell. I was off six weeks for that movie. What was it like working with Robert Duvall? He's a great guy, and we have become good friends. When we were filming *The Apostle*, I was having some medical issues. Bobby had my wife sit in a chair placed next to mine for the entire filming of the movie. 'If you see Ricky not looking like he should, let me know and we will stop shooting until he gets better.' I couldn't believe he would do that for me. I was certainly not the star of the movie."

I then asked about John Travolta.

"Travolta," he continued, "was a little standoffish at first, but once he got to know me, he was a real hoot!"

Dial also said, "Billy Bob and I continue to be good friends. I spoke to him just yesterday, and he told me that he had had strong reservations about my acting abilities during the filming of *Sling Blade*, but he wanted very much to give me a chance, and he always said, 'Rick, you can do this!'—even though he was worried to death I couldn't."

At this point, I told Dial that it took courage to be a friend of a unique kid like Thornton, but that it sure had paid off.

"Tell me about it!" he said. "On just the money I made on *Sling Blade*, I paid for my son's college education. In fact, I just got another royalty check yesterday for that movie which was made back in 1996!"

After that most interesting and revealing interview, I set up a security detail, and we made our tour.

Author's note: On Friday, May 27, 2011, Rick Dial passed away quite suddenly. Arkansas lost an outstanding native son, and Hollywood mourned his death along with his Arkansas family and friends.

James Doohan

I once had a brief encounter with Chief Engineer James Doohan of the Starship Enterprise. I was with him at an autograph table. I was very surprised that he did not sound like his character "Scotty" of *Star Trek*. I detected none of the Scottish accent that I was so accustomed to, and I discovered that he was not from Scotland, but from Canada.

Duh! He is an actor, and that was just part of his character! He was a very friendly person and openly answered questions about the other cast members in the show—with the exception of Captain Kirk (William Shatner).

I have heard Shatner talk about the rift between the two. Doohan shared some stories about it with me, but I will keep them private.

I have since read that Shatner said that he tried to make peace with Mr. Doohan to no avail. James Doohan died a few years ago, and he asked that his ashes be spread in space.

Live long and prosper in the next world, Mr. Scott. In Shatner's own words, "Scotty got beamed up!"

Winthrop Rockefeller

One day I received a call from the chief of security for one of the richest men in America, billionaire Winthrop

Rockefeller. Mr. Rockefeller was the grandson of John D. Rockefeller. He was listed in *Forbes* magazine as one of the two hundred richest men in the world.

The chief said that Mr. Rockefeller had heard about me and wanted him to train with me on the new side-handle baton. Since I was already scheduled for a class at a local police department, I told the chief it would be fine.

The chief arrived and, to my surprise, brought Mr. Rockefeller over and introduced him to me and said that Mr. Rockefeller would like to take the class as well.

"Mr. Rockefeller," I asked, "are you sure you want to do this? I thought this was just for your security chief. It can get kind of rough, and I can't go easy on you in front of the other guys."

He smiled, "No pain, no gain!"

So the training began, and it was one of the best classes I have ever had. At first, the other students were a little leery, but once they saw that Mr. Rockefeller was a serious student, they all had a good time. (I guess it didn't hurt that he offered to buy lunch for everyone.)

"Mr. Rockefeller," I later said, "right now you are a student like everyone else, and no one expects you to buy lunch, but it was a nice gesture."

In the end, we all had a good time, and it didn't hurt a thing that he made the generous offer to feed the entire class.

During breaks, Mr. Rockefeller and I talked. "Fred," he confided in me, "deep down, I have always wanted to be a cop. I've often wished I had not been born rich so I could be a street cop like you."

And I have to admit that my wishes might have been the reverse of his—to be rich. Mr. Rockefeller graduated from the class, and I signed his certificate just like everyone .else's. He was now certified to carry his new baton. Although he never became a cop, he did become a lieutenant governor and was a state police commissioner. He was also a friend of law enforcement and donated thousands of dollars to many police and corrections causes.

At his untimely death in 2006, he was worth almost $2 billion. His daughter, Andrea, of course has been rich her entire life. I am certain she became close to becoming a billionaire after her father died.

But this hasn't stopped her from working. If you happen to be driving through Arkansas, drive carefully. If you do get a speeding ticket, it might be at the hands of Officer Andrea Rockefeller. While she might only be making about $50,000 a year as a sheriff's deputy, she is serious about her job. I also don't think a bribe would work. Like father, like daughter. Money's not everything.

In Closing

I have protected many other people throughout the years. I have protected many popular singing groups, sports figures, entertainers, and business clients. All have a story to tell. Some I may tell in my next book, but many have stories I will not repeat, as this is the trust I give my clients. I have tried to make this an entertaining, fun, learning experience for the reader. I call it "enter-train-ment."

The years, though, have ticked by. As of this writing, I have over thirty-four years of service. I am semi-retired from the bodyguard business because of the long hours and because my back and feet can no longer take the strain of a long event. I still have my day job in law enforcement.

I still teach at the academy and for other law enforcement agencies and businesses. I am a keynote speaker and Special Interest Speaker on various cruise lines, traveling the world.

I still will do a short event if requested by friends. Mostly, though, I recommend others. As I review the past years, I stand amazed at the events I have seen and the history I have stood next to. I have been honored and blessed to have come from the unemployment line to the rope line with presidents and celebrities. I would have given my life for all of them, and I have learned something about life from each of them. I am also honored that you took a few minutes out of your life to work with me on this detail. I think we did pretty well. No one was hurt and we all got home safe. As Kevin Costner said in the movie *The Bodyguard*, "No one was hurt on our shift." See you on our next assignment or at my next seminar. *Live long and prosper.*

Dr. Fred Campbell

SPEAKING IN ONE OF MY SEMINARS

For lively, fun and informative seminar presentations, management training, or keynote address speaker, please contact Dr. Fred Campbell at fredwcampbell@ hotmail.com.

Bodyguard To The Stars

Made in the USA
Charleston, SC
21 December 2012